Fuck You-Aloha-I l

Wesleyan Poetry

Fuck You-Aloha-
I Love You

Juliana Spahr

Wesleyan University Press
Middletown, Connecticut

Published by Wesleyan University Press,

Middletown, CT 06459

www.wesleyan.edu/wespress

Copyright © 2001 by Juliana Spahr

Printed in the United States of America

5 4 3

Text design by Dean Bornstein

Library of Congress Cataloging-in-Publication Data

Spahr, Juliana.
  Fuck you-aloha-I love you / Juliana Spahr.
    p. cm.
  ISBN 0-8195-6524-5 (alk. paper)—ISBN 0-8195-6525-3
(pbk. : alk. paper)
  1. Hawaii—Poetry. I. Title.
  PS3569.P3356 F83 2001
  811'.54—dc21
                              2001001811

contents

acknowledgments

Different and same versions of some of
these poems have appeared in *Chicago Re-
view, Explosive Magazine, Object, Primary
Writing, Torque,* and *XCP*. Thanks to the
editors.

Thanks to Bill Luoma and Charles
Weigl. Thanks to Ranny Bledsoe, Tony
Cape, and Laurie Dahlberg for comments
on "Switching" during the Institute for
Writing and Thinking workshop. Thanks
to Cynthia Franklin and Mark Nowak.

Parts of this book were published under
the subpoetics self-publish or perish initia-
tive in June of 1998 in an edition of around
40 copies and given to friends. Thanks to
subpoetics.

For illustrations and text on final page, I
am indebted to Otto E. Ryser's *A Teacher's
Manual for Tumbling and Apparatus Stunts*.

Fuck You-Aloha-I Love You

localism or t/here

for Susan Schultz

There is no there there anywhere.
There is no here here or anywhere either.
Here and there. He and she. There, there.

Oh yes. We are lost there and here.
And here and there we err.
And we are that err.
And we are that lost.
And we are arrows of loving lostness
    gliding, gliding, off, and off, and off,
    gliding.
And arrows of unloving lostness getting
    stuck even while never hitting the
    mark.
And we are misunderstanding fullness and
    emptiness.
And we are missing our bed and all its com-
    forts that come night after night
    without end and sometimes during
    the day also and are singular even
    when coupled, doubled, and tripled
    and have something to do with the
    comforter's down coming from the
    duck.

Oh here, you are all that we want.
Oh here, come here.
You are rich and dark with soil.
And you are encouraging of growing.
And you are a soft rain without complaint
    that refreshes and stimulates.

And you are full of seeds.
And you are as accepting of the refrigerator
        as you are of the bough loaded with
        fruit.
And you and you and you are here and
        there and there and here and you are
        here and there and tear.

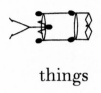

things

•

There are these things and they
are da kine to me.

There are these things and they
are clover-like.

There are these things and they
are three fold at least.

They are da kine.

They are things; they are more.

●

There are these things and they
are da kine to me. They are the tear.
The torn circle.

There are these things and they are
the circle malformed, pulled tight
in one place. These things are the
symbol of all not being right. They
are da kine for me.

Da kine for me is the moment when
things extend beyond you and me
and into the rest of the world. It is
the thing.

Like two who love each other
breaking eye contact and coming
out of that love and back into the
conversation.

The tear dropping into the water
as circle after circle resonates out.

Da kine is to be steady as a stool
on an uneven floor.

•

Da kine.

Like the claim made by astronauts
that when they see the world from
space perspective shifts.

There are these things and they are
da kine, they are the world seen from
space as whole yet complex.

The astronauts claim realizing da
kine, overwhelmed by emotion,
 an epiphany that things are fragile
from far away and thus all the more
sweet.

Da kine. Things.

●

Things that are steady as a three
legged stool on an uneven floor.

Da kine of two people coming out
and back into the conversation like
an elaborate knot that is being made.

Or the circle pulled tight in one
place to make the tear drop.

Da kine of sadness.

The symbol.

•

There are these things that are
important to me and they speak of
how all is not right with the world
yet still all is right.

At the hardcore show the singer
was screaming fuck-you-aloha-I-
love-you-fuck-you-aloha-I-love-
you.

•

The tear refers to an ideal circle that is
not met.

The tear is not right or circular.

Yet it is capable. It is da kine.

Clowns paint this wrong circle beneath
their eye because they too are pulled out
of whack.

They are the human wearing the signs
of how all is not right (the frown) yet
how things will be all right (the colorful
clothes).

Da kine.

Like fuck-you-aloha-I-love-you.

That is da kine.

•

Da kine is the mosh pit at the fuck-you-
aloha-I-love-you show.

The mosh pit is thrashing about in
masking tape.

Everyone is connected in the thrash,
everyone taped together in the fuck-
you-aloha-I-love-you.

So the thrash in anger is the thrash of
connection, of joining.

The more thrashing, the more sticking.

It is the thrash of reaching out for others
in the most isolated land mass.

It is da kine.

•

Da kine is the tear that the incarcerated
tattoo, one drop for each year caged, or
one drop for each man killed, beneath
their eye.

Here the tear is a wrong made sad yet a
defiance of this sadness.

It is worn for all to see, it is permanent
and will leave with the incarcerated
upon release, to remind us that all is not
well and that all tears are not cathartic.

So da kine is complex and the word
means anything and that is what is
lovely about it.

As lovely as a tattoo tear.

•

I am trying to tell about things,
about da kine.

Moments of looking up and out,
opening up the chest after looking
down all day.

There are these things.

Words that flip switches.

I am trying to say how they work
in a world that I am close with.

I am in a place called there and I
am trying to make it into a place
called here.

It is da kine which is saving me
always no matter where I am.

Da kine is the uneven moments
for me.

I am trying to tell you how I want
da kine. I want fuck-you-aloha-I-
love-you.

And I am reaching, reaching,
reaching for them always. For da
kine. I am reaching.

gathering
palolo stream

●

A place allows certain things.

A place allows certain things
and certain of we of a specific
place have certain rights.

●

To go to the stream is a right for
certain people.

To go, to gather.

•

The stream is a right.

It is a place for gathering.

A place for gathering āholehole

or for gathering guava, mīkana,
maiʻa

or for gathering palapalai.

•

The stream is many things.

Is busted television and niu.

Is rat and kī.

Is mongoose and freshwater.

Is ʻawa and kukui.

•

Beside the stream is a parking lot.

Yet there is no road into the
parking lot.

•

The parking lot is surrounded by
buildings on two sides

by a fence on a third

by a stream on the fourth.

•

Where the road once was is now
a parking lot for a rental space
business.

The rental space business has
surrounded their parking lot with
a high fence.

The fence gets locked at night.

•

This is about how certain of we
have rights on paper yet not in
place.

Certain of we have a right to a
gathering of the stream.

•

While the parking lot is unused,

while the stream is rich and full,

the parking lot represents the
general feeling of the space.

There is the parking lot of
limited space

the parking lot of owned by
certain of we

the parking lot of no possibility of
use

the parking lot of being unable to
park

the parking lot of growing from
the stream of gathering's freshness
of water

the parking lot beneath the
highway beside the stream of
gathering.

•

It is because certain of we are
always driving that the parking lot
matters.

Certain of we are driving to
waking up.

Certain of we are driving back
to clear ideas about what certain
of we are.

Certain of we are driving to
finishing what got interrupted.

Certain of we are driving to
orange, sticky fruit.

Certain of we are driving to the
airplane's heat shimmering off its
wings.

Certain of we are driving to clear
water moving over rocks.

Certain of we are driving to
things are this way, this way.

Certain of we are driving from
what are things.

Certain of we are driving to
waiting.

Certain of we are driving to
thinking in rooms without walls.

Certain of we are driving to
the way of it all being clear.

Certain of we are driving to
bougainvillea.

Certain of we are driving from
little cubicles, overhead lights,
bright flickering screen.

Certain of we are driving from
the way of thinking of it as one to
the way of thinking of it as one
and one.

Certain of we are driving the
metaphor.

•

The metaphor here of how we
need

and how we reach

and certain of us have rights yet
the rights are kept from certain of
us

by certain of us who are owning
place.

Certain of we have rights and
these rights are written so that
there is a possible keeping, a
keeping away, that denies
gathering.

Public Access Shoreline Hawai'i vs. Hawai'i County Planning Commission, 1995 WL 515898 protects indigenous Hawaiians traditional and customary rights of access to gather plants, harvest trees, and take game. In this decision the court said about the balance between the rights of private landowners and the rights of persons exercising traditional Hawaiian culture that "the western concept of exclusivity is not universally applicable in Hawai'i." A 1997 attempt by state legislators to regulate the law provoked large protests and was not passed. These rights, however, are constantly eroded by property owners who restrict physical access by fencing in areas, closing roads, diverting water, etc.

switching

•

In a room we sit around a table.

The table is dark wood.

It has thick legs.

It is a space for gathering with a
boundary of wood.

●

In another room, in a hotel room,
we hurriedly undress.

•

We use the table as a barrier and
we rest our things on it.

We value the table as decorum.

A table that is wood, that is hard.

•

A bed is soft and we, the two
people in the hotel room, run our
hands over each other's bodies
while reclined upon it.

We like the feel of each other's
bodies.

This is pleasure.

This is also speaking.

•

We in the room with the table
speak over the table.

We in the room with the table
gesture.

We debate how to want action.

We point.

We speak of uninvested discourse.

We confess.

We trouble.

We speak to each other in
elaborate patterns of sentences.

We are similar to each other. We
look like each other. We understand
each other even in argument.

•

We who come together with
some difficulty or we who
haven't seen each other for some
time thus desire each other all the
more on the bed in the hotel room.

This desire takes the form of one
person having one leg on one
person's shoulder and the other
leg stretched out and twined
around the other person, moving
back and forth.

•

We gather at the table to hear
opinions.

We gather at the table because we
are uncertain about what is right.

The table is where we go to
speak of uncertainty.

We gather to discuss.

We gather to pass and shuffle
papers.

We gather to use words like ethical re-
sponsibility.

We gather to advocate silence on
issues as we speak out on certain
others.

We gather to wait.

We gather to speak of our own
difficult history.

We gather to read and discuss.

We gather to puzzle.

We gather because we are similar.

We sway and are swayed.

We long for fluency.

We confess.

We trouble.

We speak again of ethical
responsibility.

Or again of uninvested discourse.

We claim rationality.

We claim what is useful or what
is not useful.

We learn.

We exchange.

This is thinking in exchange.

The love of wisdom.

•

In the hotel room we are different.

One of us is lighter, one is darker,
one is paunchy, one is thin, one is
wrinkled, one is resilient, one is
hairy, one is smooth.

These characteristics are combined
on each of us in a way.

We run our hands along each
other's bodies and have one
person with one leg on one
person's shoulder and the other
stretched out or twined around
the other person in the hotel
room.

This position is difficult.

It is not an easy position for our
bodies, our desires.

This is interaction.

This impossible position.

This position that does not even
give the most pleasure.

And yet we place all our hope in this touching.

As touching, gathering, happens in the most difficult places at the most difficult times.

•

In the room with a table we are
uncertain of what is what or
which is right.

In the room with a table, we are
heavy with things to do, things to say.
They spill out of us.

We passionately desire this space,
the table space, to be necessary.

To be productive.

The table allows us to get the
ideas of those we would not let
into our bed because they are not
darker or are not lighter or are
not paunchier or are not thinner
or are not more wrinkled or are
not more resilient or are not
hairier or are not smoother.

The table lets us get the ideas of
others and we desire this.

Yet we are unable to get comfortable
around the table.

So mainly we limit.

We limit the possibility of the
love of talking.

We say it cannot be. Or should
not be. Or must not be.

We forget the thing, the darker,
the lighter, the paunchier, the
thinner, the more wrinkled, the
more resilient, the hairier, the
 smoother in our bed together so
we can no longer tell who owns
what.

We get confused by contradictions.

We forget for this moment
interaction.

We are uncertain of action.

•

What I mean to say here is that I
am confused.

I am part of a we and then not
part of a we.

Or what I am confessing is that
when I am lost simple juxtapositions,
like comparing people in a room
with a table to people in a hotel
room, feel like sense.

Like truth feels.

What I am saying.

I am part of a we and then part of
a we.

I am confused.

I am meditating on the word we
like we all are all the time.

I am confused.

What I am saying.

I want the switching yet I am
confused.

What I am confessing.

When I am lost simple juxta-
positions seem to make sense.

This is because I am lost between
two places.

I have abandoned sureness.

•

What I am saying.

The problem is how to we all
together now.

How to speak around a table as if
one leg is on one shoulder and
then the other is stretched out or
twined around the other person.

How to get we here then together
in the same room.

How to no longer keep all our
transformative possibilities in one
small little room.

How to speak around a table as if
one leg is on one shoulder and
then the other is stretched out or
twined around the other person.

How to speaking.

How to speaking.

How to speaking as our bodies
come together and recline.

How to put one leg on one's
shoulder and then the other leg

stretched out or twined around
the other person and still enjoy
the table, the neutral, the boundary.

How to messy and can't be stopped.

How to not that one is right and
the other is wrong.

How to go to bed.

How to go to table.

We wait.

We long.

And this is it. And so it goes. And
as we move. We have learning.
This is it.

How to this is meaning.

How to work it all.

How to learned and to have
gained.

How to this is it.

How to all its forms.

•

I know this.

I am in one place and I am
longing for the geography of the
other place.

The softness or the boundary.

I am in days wanting it all.

Oh love for all.

Oh love for everything.

The moving back and forth.

Here is the way of it.

It is the way of one leg on one's
shoulder and then the other leg
stretched out or twined around
the other person.

It is the way of the mind.

Around the table we are moving,
moving.

We need the leg of our thinking
on one's shoulder and then the
other leg of our thinking

stretched out or twined around
the other person's thinking.

In the leg of our thinking we
need the table's questions, its
protections.

•

So we gain and we claim.

So we learn and so we are.

I have this thinking.

The public table thinking.

The private bed thinking.

All this putting one leg on one's
shoulder and then the other leg
stretched out or twined around
the other person is the love of
trying not to make one better
than the other.

Both need each other's rigors,
each other's practices.

Yet I am confused.

How to make meeting in invested
discourse. To make fluency. To
make flourish in both. A wrought
iron trellis in both. A place for
suspended and dangling by one's
hair in both. A place for plastic
flashing red light that represents
the heart in both. A place for love
of nature in both. A place for

cloudy, muggy day in both. A
place for detailed and intimate
writing of graffiti in the steam of
the bathroom mirror in both. The
way in both. The durable in both.
All together. Both swelling and
touching. Both listening and
changing. Both separation and
joining on the flat places of this,
our world of daily occurence.

•

Oh one of thinking.

Oh one of desiring.

Oh one of making and of doing.

This madness of love and madness
of thinking and thinking of love
and loving of thinking and loving
of maddening and thinking of
maddening.

This is the lovely part of it.

This the way we learn to thinking.

This is the way.

It is ours to keep.

It is ours.

So it might matter.

•

So we switch and the person who
has one leg on the other's shoulder
and the other leg stretched out or
twined around the other person
moves so that the other person has
one leg on the other's shoulder and
the other leg stretched out or twined
around the other person. We switch.
We switch from table to bed. So it
is what lasts if only for a moment of
coming.

•

If only for a moment.

So it is what remains.

So it is switching.

a younger man,
an older man,
and a woman

•

In the beginning, good form is
incidental.

In this thing called culture, we are
all fingers and toes. All legs and
arms.

In culture we reach out to build
ourselves.

In culture we interact.

•

In culture an older man and a
younger man stand facing each
other with their feet spread for
balance.

They place their hands on each
other's shoulders and together
they flex their knees and keep
their backs straight.

A woman steps onto their thighs,
one foot on a younger man's
thigh, one foot on an older man's
thigh.

A younger man and an older man
are support. A woman is a tower.

•

In culture woman leans her body
forward across their arms. As she
holds onto their near arms, she
places her shoulders on their far
arms. She uses them as a support.

She raises her legs off their thighs
and flexes her legs and hips
overhead. She is suspended upside
down off an older man and a
younger man.

•

In culture we have muscles and
we use these muscles to let us
move towards and on top and out
of each other.

We build ourselves into a
configuration.

We tremble as we do this.

Even after we have built, we
tremble.

•

In culture, a younger man and a
woman lie on the floor, on their
backs with their knees bent.

An older man lies across them
with his feet on a younger man's
abdomen and his head and
shoulders on a woman's abdomen.

A younger man and a woman are
steady and firm. They tilt their
heads back and raise their hips
from the floor using the tops of
their heads and bottoms of their
feet, toes spread, for support. They
lift up and support an older man.
An older man is spread across
them as a bridge is supported by
columns.

•

In culture an older man then
leans back on a woman's abdomen
and raises his body up until he is
upside down, his shoulders balanced
on a woman's abdomen. They make
a bridge with a tower.

•

As a younger man is no longer a
column of support for the bridge,
he straightens up and returns to
stand.

As an older man slowly descends
by moving his legs back over his
body and down to the ground,
raising up from a bend into a
stand.

As a woman, once an older man
has descended, slowly with her
feet spread apart straightens to
return to a stand.

•

In culture it is about a leg
moving and then another leg
moving and then the raising of
our self up with balance.

In balance a single position is
obtained and maintained for a
number of seconds before it is
discontinued.

In this maintenance we test out
the culture and see if it is useful.

It is balance that builds pyramids.

It is balance that tells us to keep
our head up and the hips and
knees well flexed.

It is balance that keeps the elbows
bent slightly and the fingers
pointing forward.

In balance, one tries to realize if
the weight is too far forward and
if so one presses downward with
the finger tips and raises the head.
Or if one realizes that the weight
is too far backward then one
presses downward with the heels
of the hands and lowers the head.

And if we lose balance, we tuck
the head and go into a forward
roll.

•

Like in culture a woman stands
with her feet apart, toes spread
for balance.

She is a support.

A younger man approaches from
one side and places his hands on
her shoulders and his feet on her
thighs.

A younger man bends at the
waist, extends off the body of a
woman.

An older man approaches from
another side and places his hands
on her shoulders and his feet on
her thigh.

An older man bends at the waist,
extends off the body of a woman.

A woman slowly rises with a
younger man and an older man at
her sides. She is straight and firm
on the ground. They are bent and
extended off of her. She carries
them up and as she rises her arms
are around a younger man's waist
and an older man's waist.

Then once she has risen, her arms
extend slowly and a younger man
and an older man slowly slide
their hands down her arms until
they are suspended by their feet,
firm and extended from her
thigh, and by their hands, their
arms reaching down touching
or almost touching the ground.

•

Culture is a group enterprise and requires the cooperation and teamwork of we who are in the formations.

There are no set patterns and innumerable combinations may be developed.

Culture uses all the available men and women.

Together we promote individual health through using our muscles with each other.

We increase our strength in the arms, shoulder girdle, chest, and upper back.

We develop neuro-physical coordination.

We are more flexible and lithe. More precise and exact.

We fall less when things are slippery.

We re-locate our bodies, get used to being whirled about.

These are our positions and we
have faith in there being many
positions.

We trust each other's bodies but
only to the extent that we can lift
ourselves off them.

•

We stand and we hold out our
arms at the side. We are a support.
We put our hands in our hands
and we raise our body up until
our body is inverted yet parallel
to our body. Our legs at our head,
our head at our knees. Our hands
in our hands. And we raise our
hands to raise us up. And we are
balanced by our hands on our
hands and our legs are in the air,
slowly spreading. We are in
motion. We are rising up into
a line.

Culture is us going up to the line
that we have made and levitating
our body off the line of our body
and making our body perpen-
dicular to our body by holding
onto the chest of our body.

We rest once we have done this.

We are inverted and yet perpen-
dicular to the ground and we are
parallel to the ground and yet
suspended above it, clinging to
we.

•

Or we build.

We build and we come and we
reach.

Our bodies are rich and various.

We continue to perform.

Our bodies are intent on lifting
and being lifted by many different
bodies.

It is like that.

We have lifted one and another
and another.

We have been lifted by one and
another and another.

So we hope to do in the future.

NOTE:

This poem uses some language from Otto E. Ryser's *A Teacher's Manual for Tumbling and Apparatus Stunts* (Dubuque, Iowa: Wm. C. Brown Company, 1951). It also draws from a performance I saw in Waikiki called "Living Sculpture," which featured three acrobats — a father, a son, and a woman — at a Las Vegas-style cabaret show called "Yes: An International Review" in the spring of 1998.

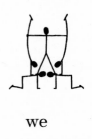

we

●

We have moved to a remote yet
populated space.

On this space things are different.
The space is known for its romantic
associations, its rich land, its beauty,
its scarce and unique resources, its
ability to grow things. Here things
grow around and into each other.

What this space feels like is that it
is the middle of the night and we are
deep asleep in our beds, dreaming.
Our we, our spouse, our mother, our
father, our caretaker, comes into the
room and turns on the light, flooding
our eyes, our minds, blinding us,
leaving us confused, lost wondering
where the dream, which feels more
solid and real than our story went.

This growing around and into
each other and the anger and the
aloha of this growing together
and around each other confuses.

•

In the midst of this unsureness,
we are trying to tell a personal
story.

This story, the story of we, is of
our loss and our loving.

It is the story between deeply
sleeping, dreaming, and waking.

It is the story of what is crooked
and loving that crooked.

•

The story goes like this: the light is
turned on and the light enters the room
and catches on the prism and the prism
fractures this light all over the room.
The prism takes the light and refracts it.
It takes the light and plays it over and
over. We are bathed in the light of the
prism, all over the room. We are bathed
in the light of waking up. This is aware-
ness. This light bathes we who are con-
cerned because we have to make room
for we who are lost or leaving other
places, we who claim land, we who
came from somewhere else, we who
are famous and followed and thus can
live anywhere we want and we want to
live here, we who are large with food
and enjoy eating, we who scribble in
notebooks and type words, we who cook
and clean, we who debate the records
and histories and offer our input and
retellings to make the swirl, we who do
elaborate dances in certain rigorously
defined styles of costumes that are many
colors and textures, we who talk late at
night in bars and consider this our cul-
tural input, we who together wear simi-
lar shirts on a certain day of the week
that define us as together, as unique, as
against a they, we who welcome the we
into our bed at night in an attempt to cut

the confusion, we who don't want to be grouped together and so loudly and determinedly give speeches denying the we, we who are I, we who want to claim an independence and superiority of our we, we who live in a certain place in a certain time and are confused about history, we who get married and married and married, we who rigorously learn a certain set of behaviors in an attempt to join something that sets us apart from those with whom we ride on the bus, we who proclaim, we who proclaim our values as culture and thus argue that these values should not be tarnished with we, we who say that is the way that it is when it might not really be that way, we who love, we who get diseases, we who get lost in the confusion, we who break down and break up, we who take drugs and drop out and say this is good, we who are sick and wasting away on hospital beds with tired loved ones beside us late at night who are wondering what we will do when the end comes, even we who are hugged by our parents who are drunk and smothering us, we who are embraced in the doorway by a lover that we never really loved and whose body embarrasses us, even we who feel the we as a part of us that makes us too big for the space we are allowed and want to shrug off this we like an oversized parka.

•

The light is we. The prism is the
space known for its romantic
associations where things grow
around and into each other. The
list of we is the prism light.

We examine the light we have
written and are confused because
we can't see the singular in it and
then we realize there is no personal
story without we.

Or if we can see a singular story
it is only for a moment as it
appears in the periphery of our
vision as a mirage while our eyes
attempt to separate the light into
its separateness and fail.

●

So we begin our personal story
with a list of who we are.

●

We want this story, our personal
story, to tell this story:

It is late at night and we lean over
and kiss, our one head one way
and our other head another way,
and stick our tongues in our
mouths and it feels strange this
way, top of tongue on top of
tongue.

A good climax to a demonstration or exhibition which includes pyramid building is the type of pyramid commonly called a "squash pyramid." The diagram above will illustrate its construction which is simple. The surprise comes in the way the pyramid collapses. At a signal, each individual in the pyramid quickly extends his arms forward and his legs backward and the pyramid simply falls in a heap. It is not at all dangerous and much simpler than it looks.